Presented To:

My Very Dear friend + sister
in the Lord, Linda

❤

From:

Dan

❤

Date:

Feb. 13, 1997
Happy Birthday

P.S. GOD LOVES YOU

Words of Grace and Encouragement
from God's Heart to Yours

by Connie Witter

Honor Books, Inc.
P.O. Box 55388
Tulsa, OK 74155

P.S. God Loves You
ISBN 1-56292-191-6
Copyright © 1996 by Connie Witter
P. O. Box 3064
Broken Arrow, Oklahoma 74013-3064

Published by Honor Books, Inc.
P.O. Box 55388
Tulsa, Oklahoma 74155

Introduction

Do you ever feel like God is a million miles away and is not listening to your prayers? The paraphrases of Scripture verses in this book are designed to remind you, or show you for the first time, that God is not only there for you, but He's interested in every aspect of your life. In fact, He wrote the Bible to tell you of His limitless, unconditional love and that He longs to share a personal, intimate relationship with you.

P.S. God Loves You will not only reveal to you God's love and acceptance, but also His desire to see you succeed and be happy. He is constantly looking for opportunities to help you achieve in life and become more content. So sit down and read the entire book and you'll be bathed in the love of God, or keep it close by to pick up when you have a low moment in your day. Either way you'll hear God whispering to you, "I love you."

When you are in confusion, wondering which way to go, remember that I have a plan for your life. Put your trust in Me and I will show you the way to go. I will bring My plans for you to pass— and I will complete them!

I will cry to God Most High, Who performs on my behalf and rewards me [Who brings to pass (His purposes) for me and surely completes them]!
PSALM 57:2 AMP

I created you in your mother's womb. I was there, watching in secret, as your body was being formed. I wrote down My plan for your life before you took your first breath. Oh, My child, how I desire that you would follow the plan that I created for you.

For you created my inmost being; you knit me together in my mother's womb. My frame was not hidden from you when I was made in the secret place. When I was woven together in the depths of the earth, your eyes saw my unformed body. All the days ordained for me were written in your book before one of them came to be.

PSALM 139:13,15,16

8

I created you for a special reason. I have prepared a specific plan just for you. It is never too late to start resting in My unfailing love and trusting your life to Me. Then I can work on your behalf, fulfilling My purpose and making you into everything I created you to be.

The Lord will fulfill his purpose for me;
your love, O Lord, endures forever—
do not abandon the works of your hands.
PSALM 138:8 NIV

For I am confident of this very thing,
that He who began a good work in you
will perfect it until the day of Christ Jesus.
PHILIPPIANS 1:6 NAS

*M*y greatest desire is for you to have the best in every area of your life. I have told you in the Bible, which is My Word to you, that I want you to succeed and be healthy as you grow in maturity and wisdom.

Beloved, I wish above all things that thou mayest prosper and be in health, even as thy soul prospereth.
3 JOHN 2 KJV

*M*y plan for you and everything I desire to do in your life is beyond what you could hope for; it is beyond what you could dream. I am able to do this as you put your trust in Me and allow the power of My Spirit to work within you.

Now to him that is able to do immeasurably
more than all we ask or imagine, according
to his power that is at work within us.
EPHESIANS 3:20

*P*ut your confidence in Me! As you depend on Me, I am at work on your behalf. I am working everything into a marvelous plan for your good, because I created you for a special purpose.

We are assured and know that
(God being a partner in their labor),
all things work together and are (fitting into a plan)
for good to those who love God and are called
according to (His) design and purpose.
ROMANS 8:28 AMP

*Y*ou are My masterpiece. I created you to accomplish great things on the earth. Everything I have for you to do I planned before the world was ever created.

For we are God's workmanship, created in Christ Jesus to do good works, which God prepared in advance for us to do.

EPHESIANS 2:10

"For I know the plans I have for you," declares the Lord, "plans to prosper you and not to harm you, plans to give you hope and a future."

JEREMIAH 29:11

*T*his is what the Lord says—your Redeemer, the Holy One of Israel; "I am the Lord your God, who teaches you what is best for you, who directs you in the way you should go."

ISAIAH 48:17

*A*s your Heavenly Father, I have placed dreams and visions within your heart. Do not become discouraged and let go of them. Your vision is for a specific time. Though it may be delayed, wait patiently for it, for you will not be disappointed. I will surely bring it to pass in My perfect timing.

For the vision is yet for the appointed time;
It hastens toward the goal, and it will not fail.
Though it tarries, wait for it;
For it will certainly come, it will not delay.
HABAKKUK 2:3 NAS

*F*ollowing My instructions for living that I have written in My Word will profit you in every way. My promised blessings are not only for heaven, but for right now on earth.

Godliness is profitable unto all things,
having promise of the life that now is,
and of that which is to come.
1 TIMOTHY 4:8 KJV

I am your Heavenly Father and I always speak the truth. I know the purpose of your life, so don't be discouraged when something you were hoping for does not occur. When the time is right, I will open a door for you, and no man will be able to close it.

These things saith he that is holy, he that is true...
I know thy works: behold, I have set before thee
an open door, and no man can shut it.
REVELATIONS 3:7,8 KJV

Do not believe the lie that I would bring harm into your life. You are My beloved child, and only that which is good comes from My hand.

Don't be deceived, my dear brothers. Every good and perfect gift is from above, coming down from the Father.

JAMES 1:16,17

I did not create you to be a failure. I created you to be a success. I have promised that if you will meditate in My Word and walk in My ways, your life will be prosperous and successful.

This book of the law shall not depart out of thy mouth;
but thou shalt meditate therein day and night,
that thou mayest observe to do
according to all that is written therein:
for then thou shalt make thy way prosperous,
and then thou shalt have good success.
Joshua 1:8 KJV

*T*ake joy in your relationship with Me. Place your life in My hands and put your confidence in Me. Then I will move in your life and satisfy the desires of your heart.

Delight thyself also in the Lord;
and he shall give thee the desires of thine heart.
Commit thy way unto the Lord;
trust also in him; and he shall bring it to pass.
PSALM 37:4,5 KJV

I will instruct you and teach you in the way you should go; I will counsel you and watch over you.

PSALM 32:8

*A*nd your ears shall hear a word behind you, saying, This is the way; walk in it, when you turn to the right hand and when you turn to the left.

ISAIAH 30:21 AMP

*L*isten, my Son, accept what I say, and the years of your life will be many. I guide you in the way of wisdom and lead you along straight paths. When you walk, your steps will not be hampered; when you run, you will not stumble.

PROVERBS 4:10–12

*B*e humble by realizing you need Me. Depend upon Me and I will exalt you and honor you. I will make your life significant.

Humble yourselves in the sight of the Lord, and he shall lift you up.
JAMES 4:10 KJV

*L*isten to My voice and follow My direction, and I will show you how to be successful in your family, your profession, and in your finances. I take the greatest pleasure in seeing you prosper.

And you shall return and obey the voice of the Lord...
And the Lord your God will make you abundantly prosperous
in every work of your hand, in the fruit of your body,
of your cattle, of your land, for good;
for the Lord will again delight in prospering you.
DEUTERONOMY 30:8,9 AMP

*E*ntrust everything you do into My hands and put your complete reliance on Me. Then I will put My thoughts in your mind, your plans will become My plans, and your success will be guaranteed.

Roll your works upon the Lord
[commit and trust them wholly to Him;
He will cause your thoughts to become
agreeable to His will, and]
so shall your plans be established
<u>and</u> succeed.
PROVERBS 16:3 AMP

*Y*ou may be thinking *you* know where you want to go, but *My* purpose for you is what will work. As my child, every step you take is ordered by Me. I am actively involved in your life, pointing you toward true success.

Many are the plans in a man's heart,
but it is the Lord's purpose that prevails.
PROVERBS 19:21

The steps of a good man are ordered by the Lord:
and he delighteth in his way.
PSALM 37:23 KJV

$\mathcal{G}$ive every concern of your heart to Me, and ask Me for guidance. Do not rely on your limited knowledge. In everything you do depend on Me, and I will show you the way to go.

Trust in the Lord with all thine heart;
and lean not unto thine own understanding.
In all thy ways acknowledge him,
and he shall direct thy paths.
PROVERBS 3:5,6 KJV

*L*ook at all the incredible things I have created, and yet you are so special and precious to Me that I am constantly thinking about you. My thoughts concerning you are too numerous to count.

Many, O Lord my God, are the wonderful works which You have done, and Your thoughts toward us; no one can compare with You! If I should declare and speak of them, they are too many to be numbered.
PSALM 40:5 AMP

I have created you and cared for you since you were born. I will be your God through all your lifetime, yes, even when your hair is white with age. I made you and I will care for you. I will carry you along and be your Savior.

ISAIAH 46:3,4 TLB

I am the Lord your God...I have put my words in your mouth and hidden you safe within my hand...I am the one who says..."You are mine."

ISAIAH 51:15,16 TLB

*M*y love for you is unconditional. No power in heaven or earth can come between us. And nothing you have done in the past, or would ever do in the future, could cause Me to withdraw My love from you.

For I am persuaded, that neither death, nor life,
nor angels, nor principalities, nor powers,
nor things present, nor things to come,
Nor height, nor depth, nor any
other creature, shall be able to
separate us from the love of God,
which is in Christ Jesus our Lord.
ROMANS 8:38,39 KJV

I am watching over you constantly. I notice everything you do and take great interest in every aspect of your life. I know you so intimately that I have numbered the hairs of your head. You have no reason to be afraid, for you are of great value to Me.

Are not two little sparrows sold for a penny?
And yet not one of them will fall to the ground without
your Father's leave (consent) and notice. But even the very
hairs of your head are all numbered. Fear not, then; you are
of more value than many sparrows.
MATTHEW 10:29-31 AMP

I know you intimately. I know what you are thinking and how you feel. Every moment, I am aware of where you are. As you walk the path of life, I will be with you and watch over you. Count your blessings and know that every one of them has come from My hand.

O Lord, you have examined my heart and know everything about me. You know when I sit or stand. When far away you know my every thought. You chart the path ahead of me and tell me where to stop and rest. Every moment you know where I am. You both precede and follow me and place your hand of blessing on my head.

PSALM 139:1-3,5 TLB

Do not be full of worry and fear. Give Me your cares and put your complete trust in Me. You are My child and I care about every area of your life. So rest in My unfailing love, and I will take care of everything that concerns you.

Cast all your anxiety on him because he cares for you.
1 PETER 5:7

The Lord will perfect that which concerns me.
PSALM 138:8 AMP

*L*ike a shepherd provides for his sheep, I will provide for you. You are special and valuable to Me. Rest in My love and I will carry you in My arms and give you great peace.

He tends his flock like a shepherd:
He gathers the lambs in his arms
and carries them close to his heart.
ISAIAH 40:11

"I myself will be the Shepherd of my sheep,
and cause them to lie down in peace," the Lord God says.
EZEKIEL 34:15 TLB

I love you with a love that will last forever. I drew you to My side and into My arms thinking only kind thoughts about you, knowing your faults and failings, yet loving you despite them. I am your Heavenly Father and I will never stop loving you.

The Lord appeared...saying:
"I have loved you with an everlasting love;
I have drawn you with loving-kindness."
JEREMIAH 31:3

"To me this is like the days of Noah, when I swore that the waters of Noah would never again cover the earth. So now I have sworn not to be angry with you, never to rebuke you again. Though the mountains be shaken and the hills be removed, yet my unfailing love for you will not be shaken nor my covenant of peace be removed," says the Lord, who has compassion on you.

ISAIAH 54:9,10

*F*orget the former things; do not dwell on the past... I, even I, am he who blots out your transgressions, for my own sake, and remembers your sins no more.

Isaiah 43:18,25

I will never forget you! You are very precious in My sight. You are so special to Me that I have imprinted your picture on the palms of My hands.

Can a woman forget her sucking child,
that she should not have compassion on the son of her womb?
Yea, they may forget, yet will I not forget thee.
Behold, I have graven thee upon the palms of <u>my</u> hands.
ISAIAH 49:15,16 KJV

I love you so much that I sacrificed My only Son for you, that you might put your trust in Him and receive eternal life.

For God so loved the world, that he gave his only begotten Son, that whosoever believeth in him should not perish, but have ever-lasting life.
JOHN 3:16 KJV

I am your Provider and your Protector. Because you put your trust in Me, I will meet all your needs. Though you walk in the midst of trouble, do not be afraid, because I am always with you. I will guide you and keep you from harm. My mercy and goodness will surround you, and you will have a home with Me forever.

The Lord is my shepherd; I shall not want.
Yea, though I walk through the valley of the shadow
of death, I will fear no evil: for thou art with me; thy rod
and thy staff they comfort me. Surely goodness and
mercy shall follow me all the days of my life: and I will
dwell in the house of the Lord for ever.

PSALM 23:1,4,6 KJV

*B*ecause of My great love for you, even when your spirit was dead because of your sins, I made it alive when you accepted My Son as your Lord. You do not have to earn salvation. Eternal life is My free gift to you when you place your faith in My Son Jesus.

But because of his great love for us, God,
who is rich in mercy, made us alive with Christ
even when we were dead in transgressions—
it is by grace you have been saved.
EPHESIANS 2:4,5

The gift of God is eternal life in Christ Jesus our Lord.
ROMANS 6:23

I have given you My ability and wisdom, in My Spirit and My Word, to live a fulfilled life of victory. As you pursue an intimate relationship with Jesus, the joy and integrity of your life will glorify Me.

According as his divine power hath given unto us
all things that pertain unto life and godliness,
through the knowledge of him
that hath called us to glory and virtue.
2 Peter 1:3 KJV

*T*hrough your new life in Jesus, I have given you awesome and life-changing promises. As you put your trust in them, you will become more and more like Me, and then My strength and wisdom will enable you to resist all temptation. This will give you a life full of love, joy, and peace.

Whereby are given unto us exceeding great and precious promises: that by these ye might be partakers of the divine nature, having escaped the corruption that is in the world through lust.

2 PETER 1:4 KJV

*B*ut no weapon that is formed against you shall prosper, and every tongue that shall rise against you in judgment you shall show to be in the wrong. This [peace, righteousness, security, triumph over opposition] is the heritage of the servants of the Lord.

ISAIAH 54:17 AMP

*C*ome to Me, all you who are weary and burdened, and I will give you rest. Take my yoke upon you and learn from me, for I am gentle and humble in heart, and you will find rest for your souls.

MATTHEW 11:28,29

I will never stop loving you, nor will I ever break My promises. I will not violate the contract that was sealed in Jesus' blood, and I will never change My mind. So put your faith and trust in Me, and you will never be disappointed; for I am faithful to My Word.

But I will not take my love from him,
nor will I ever betray my faithfulness.
I will not violate my covenant or alter
what my lips have uttered.
PSALMS 89:33,34

He who promised is faithful.
HEBREWS 10:23

*M*ore than anything else, I want you to know how great My love is for you. It goes beyond your human understanding, but you can grasp the reality of My love as you read My Word and consider all that I have done. As you are filled with My love, you will enjoy your life to the fullest.

I pray that you, being rooted and established in love, may have power, together with all the saints, to grasp how wide and long and high and deep is the love of Christ, and to know this love that surpasses knowledge—that you may be filled to the measure of all the fullness of God.

EPHESIANS 3:17-19

49

When you feel weak, draw on My power within you. Then I will make you strong! There is *nothing* you cannot do when you put your trust in Me. You can do *all* things through Jesus Christ, Who gives you supernatural strength when you need it.

I have strength for all things in Christ Who empowers me—
[I am ready for anything and equal to anything through Him
Who infuses inner strength into me,
that is, I am self-sufficient in Christ's sufficiency].
PHILIPPIANS 4:13 AMP

Why do you choose to go your own way instead of Mine? Why do you worry instead of having faith in my promises? But even when you run from Me, I continue to pursue you. How I desire to bless you, if only you would seek My unbroken companionship.

In repentance and rest is your salvation, in quietness and trust is your strength, but you would have none of it....Yet the Lord longs to be gracious to you; he rises to show you compassion. For the Lord is a God of justice. Blessed are all who wait for him!

ISAIAH 30:15,18

When you pray, I hear you! Not only do I hear you, but I will answer you, and you will be in awe of My great love. I will move strong in your life as you depend on Me. You are the apple of My eye, and I send My angels to protect you.

I call on you, O God, for you will answer me; give ear to me and hear my prayer. Show the wonder of your great love, you who save by your right hand those who take refuge in You from their foes. Keep me as the apple of your eye; hide me in the shadow of your wings.

PSALM 17:6,8

*Y*ou are never alone My child; for I am your Heavenly Father, and I will always be there to help you in your time of need.

God is our refuge and strength,
an ever-present help in trouble.
PSALM 46:1

*B*ecause you have made the Lord your refuge, and the Most High your dwelling place, there shall no evil befall you, nor any plague or calamity come near your tent. For He will give His angels (especial) charge over you to accompany *and* defend *and* preserve you in all your ways....

PSALM 91:9-11 AMP

My son, do not forget my teaching, but keep my commands in your heart, for they will prolong your life many years and bring you prosperity.

PROVERBS 3:1,2

I earnestly search the earth for those who trust in My promises, that I might prove My love and faithfulness to them. You are one of those whom I seek, so depend upon Me, and I will do a powerful work in your life.

For the eyes of the Lord run to and
fro throughout the whole earth,
to shew himself strong in the
behalf of them whose heart is
perfect toward him.

2 CHRONICLES 16:9 KJV

When you are in trouble, run to Me, and I will be your fortress of safety. I will help you and deliver you when you put your trust in Me.

The salvation of the righteous comes from the Lord;
he is their stronghold in time of trouble. The Lord
helps them and delivers them; he delivers
them from the wicked and saves them,
because they take refuge in him.

PSALM 37:39,40

I have clearly shown My great love for you by the fact that while you were still a sinner, I sent My Son to die in your place. I have forgiven you for all your sins through the blood of Jesus. Now you are no longer under My wrath. You are under My grace!

But God demonstrates his own love for us in this: While we were still sinners, Christ died for us. Since we have now been justified by his blood, how much more shall we be saved from God's wrath through him!

ROMANS 5:8,9

I am always watching you. I pay attention to your cry for help. When you call to Me in times of trouble, I will bring you through your trial victoriously.

The eyes of the Lord are on the righteous
and his ears are attentive to their cry.
The righteous cry out, and the Lord hears them;
he delivers them from all their troubles.

PSALM 34:15,17

When you accepted My Son Jesus as your Savior, you became a new person on the inside. Your old sins, mistakes, and attitudes have been forgiven, and I have forgotten them. You have a brand new life!

Therefore if any man be in Christ,
he is a new creature: old things are
passed away; behold, all things
are become new.
2 CORINTHIANS 5:17 KJV

*F*orget the past!   Give all your energy and talent to fulfilling My purpose for your life. Press on toward all that I have called you to do, and you will have great rewards waiting for you in heaven.

Forgetting what lies behind and reaching forward
to what lies ahead, I press on toward the goal for
the prize of the upward call of God in Christ Jesus.
PHILIPPIANS 3:13,14 NAS

*B*ut now the Lord who created you...says: Don't be afraid, for I have ransomed you; I have called you by name; you are mine. When you go through deep waters and great trouble, I will be with you. When you go through rivers of difficulty, you will not drown! When you walk through the fire of oppression, you will not be burned up—the flames will not consume you. For I am the Lord your God, your Savior....

ISAIAH 43:1-3 TLB

*F*ear not; [there is nothing to fear] for I am with you; do not look around you in terror *and* be dismayed, for I am your God. I will strengthen *and* harden you [to difficulties]; yes, I will help you; yes, I will hold you up *and* retain you with My [victorious] right hand....

ISAIAH 41:10 AMP

My child, you will face many problems in life, but take courage and be confident; for I am your Heavenly Father and I have promised to deliver you out of them all!

A righteous man may have many troubles, but the Lord delivers him from them all.

PSALM 34:19

As your Heavenly Father, all I require of you is that you would reverence Me. This means to walk in My ways, to love Me, and to serve Me with all your heart. Then I can pour My blessings into your life, which is My greatest delight.

What does the Lord your God require of you, but [reverently] to fear the Lord your God (that is) to walk in all His ways and to love Him, and to serve the Lord your God with all your [mind and] heart and with your entire being. To keep the commandments of the Lord, and His statutes, which I command you today for your good?
DEUTERONOMY 10:12,13 AMP

I know that you love Me because you trust and obey My Word. Therefore, I will deliver you in times of trouble. When you cry for help, I will answer. I will rescue you and esteem you. I will bless you with a long life and cause you to come through every trial victoriously.

"Because he loves me," says the Lord, "I will rescue him;
I will protect him, for he acknowledges my name. He will call
upon Me, and I will answer him; I will be with him in trouble,
I will deliver him and honor him. With long life will I satisfy
him and show him my salvation."

PSALM 91:14–16

I know the troubles you are facing. Come to Me with confidence, because you are My beloved child. Then I will give you mercy for your failures and grace to overcome in your time of need.

*Let us then approach the throne of grace
with confidence, so that we may receive mercy
and find grace to help us in our time of need.*
HEBREWS 4:16

*I*f I sacrificed My only Son so you could become My child, why would you ever doubt that I would withhold any blessing from you? I take great pleasure in freely and generously giving you everything you need.

He who did not spare his own Son,
but gave him up for us all—
how will he not also, along with him,
graciously give us all things?
ROMANS 8:32

Do not seek revenge on those who have made you suffer by their words or deeds. Instead, speak kindly to them. Bless them by praying for them and being truly loving and compassionate. If you do this, nothing can hinder you from receiving My blessings in every area of your life.

Never return evil for evil or insult for insult...but on the contrary blessing—[praying for their welfare, happiness and protection, and truly pitying and loving them]: For know that to this you have been called, that you may yourselves inherit a blessing [from God—that you may obtain a blessing as heirs, bringing welfare and happiness and protection].

1 PETER 3:9 AMP

*F*or I am the Lord, your God, who takes hold of your right hand and says to you, Do not fear; I will help you.

ISAIAH 41:13

*H*e [God] Himself has said, I will not in any way fail you *nor* give you up *nor* leave you without support. [I will] not, [I will] not, [I will] not in any degree leave you helpless, *nor* forsake *nor* let [you] down (relax My hold on you)!— [Assuredly Not!]

HEBREW 13:5 AMP

*B*uild your marriage, your family, and your life on the wisdom of My Word! It is a firm and sound foundation that will never fail you. Follow My counsel and every area of your life will be filled with awesome riches and satisfaction.

Through skillful <u>and</u> godly Wisdom is a house (a life, a home, a family) built, and by understanding it is established [on a sound and good foundation]. And by knowledge shall the chamber [of its every area] be filled with all precious and pleasant riches.

PROVERBS 24:3,4 AMP

*J*take great pleasure in you when you trust Me and honor My Word. I rejoice when you put your hope in My unconditional love. I promise, you will never be disappointed when you put your hope in Me.

The Lord delights in those who fear him,
who put their hope in his unfailing love.
PSALM 147:11

Then you will know that I am the Lord;
those who hope in me will not be disappointed.
ISAIAH 49:23

*B*ecause I do not want you to live in fear, I have given you a spirit filled with My power, My love, and a calm, stable mind. Put your trust in Me, remembering My faithfulness, and I will surround you with peace.

For God has not given us a spirit of fear,
but of power and of love and of a sound mind.
2 TIMOTHY 1:7 NKJ

Thou wilt keep him in perfect peace, whose mind
is stayed on thee: because he trusteth in thee.
ISAIAH 26:3 KJV

My child, do not rely on your own wisdom, but have deep reverence toward Me and turn entirely away from evil. This will bring health and strength to your body.

Do not be wise in your own eyes; fear the Lord and shun evil. This will bring health to your body and nourishment to your bones.

PROVERBS 3:7,8

75

*D*o not forget all the benefits of being My child! Not only have I promised to forgive all your sins, but I have also promised to heal all of your diseases.

Praise the Lord, O my soul, and forget not all his benefits—
who forgives all your sins and heals all your diseases.

PSALM 103:2,3

*D*o you not realize what My Son Jesus did for you? He was beaten and crucified to pay the price for your sin. He took your punishment to give you peace and prosperity. And He bore stripes on His back so that you might be healed.

But He was wounded for our transgressions,
He was bruised for our guilt and
iniquities; the chastisement needful to
obtain peace and well-being for us
was upon Him, and with the stripes that
wounded Him we are healed and made whole.
ISAIAH 53:5 AMP

*M*y son, attend to my words; consent and submit to my sayings. Let them not depart from your sight; keep them in the center of your heart. For they are life to those who find them, healing and health to all their flesh.

PROVERBS 4:20-22 AMP

"But I will restore health to you and heal your wounds," declares the Lord.

JEREMIAH 30:17

I am the Lord that healeth thee.

EXODUS 15:26 KJV

I want you to understand this truth: When you care more about pleasing others than pleasing Me, you open the door for destruction in your life. Always remember My love for you is greater than what any man could ever say or do to you. Choose to trust in Me, My child, and you will always dwell in safety and be successful.

The fear of man brings a snare, but whoever leans on, trusts, and puts his confidence in the Lord is safe and set on high.
PROVERBS 29:25 AMP

*D*o not try to be perfect by depending on yourself! Stop struggling to please Me in your own strength. Put your trust in My ability and ask Me to strengthen you, and I will create in you the power and desire to do those things that are pleasing in My sight.

(Not in your own strength) for it is God Who is all the while effectually at work in you—energizing and creating in you the power and desire—both to will and to work for His good pleasure and satisfaction and delight.

Philippians 2:13 AMP

Keep your eyes on Me and put your trust in what I have promised. You will be blessed, happy, and fortunate as you rely on Me.

O Lord of hosts, How blessed is the man who trusts in Thee!
PSALM 84:12 NAS

*L*earn about My grace by reading, studying, and meditating on My Word. My Word is able to strengthen you to live a holy, victorious life, which is your inheritance as My child. I have set you apart, as I have all My children, in order to love and bless you.

*Now I commit you to God and to the word of his grace,
which can build you up and give you an inheritance
among all those who are sanctified.*

ACTS 20:32

Don't become insensitive to My Spirit or take My Word for granted. But imitate those who have faith in My promises and persevere in the knowledge that My timing is perfect. Do not lose interest—stay focused—and you will inherit what I have promised in My Word.

That ye be not slothful, but followers of them who through faith and patience inherit the promises.
HEBREWS 6:12 KJV

*D*o not weaken in faith when you consider your circumstances. Do not waiver or question My promises to you. Follow the example of your father Abraham, and become empowered by faith as you begin to thank Me for the answer, knowing without a doubt that I will bring to pass all I have promised.

And being not weak in faith, he considered not his own body now dead,...He staggered not at the promise of God through unbelief; but was strong in faith, giving glory to God; And being fully persuaded that, what he had promised, he was able also to perform.

ROMANS 4:19-21 KJV

*Y*ou are precious to me and honored, and I love you. All who claim me as their God will come, for I have made them for my glory; I created them.

ISAIAH 43:4,7 TLB

*B*efore I formed you in the womb I knew you,
before you were born I set you apart.

JEREMIAH 1:5

*T*here has never been another god like Me, because I truly care about you and everything you are going through. I see your situation. I know your heart's desire, and I am willing to move powerfully on your behalf. Trust Me; I am able.

For from of old, men have not heard, nor perceived by the ear,
nor has the eye seen a God besides You, Who works
and shows Himself active on behalf of him
who (earnestly) waits for Him.

ISAIAH 64:4 AMP

*D*o not let go of the hope you cherish and confess. Seize it and hold it tight. Put your hope in what I have promised you; for I am reliable, trustworthy, and faithful to My Word.

*Let us hold unswervingly to
the hope we profess,
for he who promised is faithful.*
HEBREWS 10:23

*P*ut your faith in My Word and you will walk in victory. You will be an overcomer in every situation, for I have made you more than a conqueror through Christ Jesus.

For everyone born of God overcomes the world. This is the victory that has overcome the world, even our faith.
1 JOHN 5:4

We are more than conquerors through him who loved us.
ROMANS 8:37

*H*ow I long for you to feel My presence. As you thank Me and praise Me for all I do throughout the day and remember all I have done through My Son Jesus, you will live and abide in My presence, and your life will overflow with My joy.

Enter into his gates with thanksgiving,
<u>and</u> into his courts with praise:
be thankful unto him, <u>and</u> bless his name.
PSALM 100:4 KJV

In Your presence is fullness of joy,
at Your right hand are pleasures for evermore.
PSALM 16:11 AMP

*W*hen you come to Me in prayer, do not come on the basis of who you are or what you have done. Come on the basis of what My Son Jesus did for you, and I will gladly bless you.

*But all who humble themselves before the Lord
shall be given every blessing....*
PSALM 37:11 TLB

*For we (Christians)...who worship God in spirit...exult and
glory and pride ourselves in Jesus Christ, and put no
confidence or dependence (on what we are) in the flesh....*
PHILIPPIANS 3:3 AMP

I sent My Son Jesus to pay the price for your sins. He loved you so much, He was willing to take your punishment for being unable to keep all My commands. When you put your trust in Him as your Savior, My Spirit comes to dwell in your heart, and I bless you in the same way I blessed Abraham.

Christ redeemed us from the curse of the law by becoming a curse for us...he redeemed us in order that the blessing given to Abraham might come to the Gentiles through Christ Jesus, so that by faith we might receive the promise of the Spirit.

GALATIANS 3:13,14

*S*o is my word that goes out from my mouth: It will not return to me empty, but will accomplish what I desire and achieve the purpose for which I sent it.

ISAIAH 55:11

*F*or I am alert and active, watching over My Word to perform it.

JEREMIAH 1:12 AMP

*F*or I am the Lord; I will speak, and the word that I shall speak shall be performed—come to pass; it shall be no more delayed or prolonged... I will speak the word and I will perform it, says the Lord God.

EZEKIEL 12:25 AMP

*D*o not consider the Bible as the writings of men, but as what it really is—My Word to you! When you believe it is My Word and put your absolute trust in it, you will experience My supernatural ability in your life.

When you received the message of God...
you welcomed it not as the word of (mere) men but as what it
truly is, the Word of God, which is effectually at work
in you who believe—exercising its (superhuman)
power in those who adhere to and trust
in and rely on it.
1 THESSALONIANS 2:13 AMP

Do you not realize how much I love you? If you, as an earthly parent, want the best for your children, how much more do I as your Heavenly Father want the best for you? I delight in giving you good things when you ask Me.

If ye then, being evil, know how to give good gifts unto your children, how much more shall your Father which is in heaven give good things to them that ask him?
MATTHEW 7:11 KJV

97

*Y*ou can trust Me completely! I would never lie to you. What I have spoken, I will perform. What I have promised, I will fulfill. Put your trust in My Word, for I am faithful to all of My promises.

God is not a man, that he should lie, nor a son of man,
that he should change his mind. Does he speak
and then not act? Does he promise and not fulfill?
NUMBERS 23:19

The Lord is faithful to all his promises
and loving toward all he has made.
PSALM 145:13

*C*ome to Me in prayer and remind Me of My promises. When you ask for anything I have promised in My Word, My answer to you will always be "Yes!" because of Jesus. So confidently respond to My answer by saying, "Amen, so be it in my life!" Your life will glorify Me when you partake of all that I have promised.

You who (are his servants and by your prayers)
put the Lord in remembrance (of his promises).
Isaiah 62:6 AMP

For no matter how many promises God has made,
they are "Yes" in Christ. And so through him the "Amen"
is spoken by us to the glory of God.
2 Corinthians 1:20

*L*ive in My Word! Conform your life to what I have said and draw your life from Me. Then, as My Word remains real and alive in your heart, you will pray according to My will and whatever you ask will be accomplished.

If ye abide in me, and my words abide in you, ye shall ask what ye will, and it shall be done unto you.
JOHN 15:7 KJV

*I*n My word I have revealed to you My will for every area of your life. Therefore, this is the confidence that you can have in Me. If you ask Me for anything in agreement with My Word, I will hear your prayer. And if you know that I hear you, you can also know that I will give you the petition that you requested.

This is the confidence we have in approaching God: that if we ask anything according to his will, he hears us. And if we know that he hears us—whatever we ask—we know that we have what we asked of him.

1 JOHN 5:14,15

*A*nd whatever you ask for in prayer, having faith and (really) believing, you will receive.

MATTHEW 21:22 AMP

I am the Lord, the God of all mankind. Is anything too hard for me?

JEREMIAH 32:27

*D*o not become discouraged! Your situation may seem impossible in the natural, but if you put your hope in Me, I am able to change your circumstances. Nothing is impossible if you only believe.

Why are you downcast, O my soul? Why so disturbed within me? Put your hope in God.
PSALM 42:5

All things are possible to him who believes.
MARK 9:23 NAS

*A*bsolutely no situation is impossible for Me to work out for you. No promise that I have made in My Word is without power, for I am able and willing to perform it in your life.

*For with God nothing is ever impossible,
and no word from God shall be without power
or impossible of fulfillment.*
LUKE 1:37 AMP

*A*sk for anything in the name of Jesus and I will give it to you. I delight in answering your prayers so that your heart might rejoice in My faithfulness.

I tell you the truth, my father will give you whatever you ask in my name. Until now you have not asked for anything in my name. Ask and you will receive, and your joy will be complete.

JOHN 16:23,24

I gave My promises to Abraham and to His children. When you put your faith in Jesus, you became My child and Abraham's seed. Thus, all of My promises to Abraham now belong to you.

Now to Abraham and his seed were the promises made....
And if ye <u>be</u> Christs, then are ye Abraham's seed,
and heirs according to the promise.
GALATIANS 3:16,29 KJV

When you worship Me, remember that I have promised you joy, peace, health, prosperity, victory, success, and protection. When you trust in My promises, I will be faithful to perform them in your life, for the integrity of My name is at stake.

I face your Temple as I worship, giving thanks to you for all your loving-kindness and your faithfulness, for your promises are backed by all the honor of your name.
PSALM 138:2 TLB

I have come to you and given you My Word so that you could have My joy. You will have My gladness within you, filling your heart, when you live and abide in My Word.

And now come I to thee; and these things I speak in the world, that they might have my joy fulfilled in themselves.

JOHN 17:13 KJV

*T*he Spirit gives life; the flesh counts for nothing. The words I have spoken to you are spirit and they are life.

JOHN 6:63

*I*f you abide in My Word—hold fast to My teachings and live in accordance with them—you are truly My disciples. And you will know the truth, and the truth will set you free.

JOHN 8:31,32 AMP

*H*ow I desire that you would live a life of abundance. I have promised that as you delight in My Word and meditate upon it day and night, you will be like a tree planted near the rivers of living water. You will live a productive life, and everything you do will succeed.

Blessed is the man...[whose] delight is in the law of the Lord, and on his law he meditates day and night. He is like a tree planted by streams of water, which yields its fruit in season and whose leaf does not whither.
Whatever he does prospers.

PSALM 1:1-3

*T*he thief would like to kill, steal, and destroy you. But I sent My Son Jesus so that you might be protected and walk in abundant life, enjoying it to the fullest.

The thief cometh not, but for to steal, and to kill, and to destroy: I am come that they might have life, and that they might have it more abundantly.
JOHN 10:10 KJV

*Y*ou can rest assured that I am helping you become all I have created you to be. I will never stop working in you, strengthening you to perform the plan I have for your life until the day My Son Jesus returns to earth.

Being confident of this, that he who began a good work in you will carry it on to completion until the day of Christ Jesus.
PHIPPIANS 1:6

*A*s you give generously, I will bless you abundantly. When you give cheerfully, it pleases Me, and I will gladly give you more than you need. Then you will have the abundance to bless others, by supporting those who preach and teach My Word and by taking care of those in need.

Whoever sows generously will also reap generously...
for God loves a cheerful giver.... And God is able to make all
grace abound toward you, so that in all things at all times,
having all that you need, you will abound in every good work.

2 CORINTHIANS 9:6–8

$\mathscr{B}$e careful not to become arrogant when I bless you abundantly. Nor should you trust in all I have given you, because riches are not dependable, and they can never bring you true happiness. But as you depend on Me, you will be able to fully enjoy all of My blessings.

Command those who are rich in this present world not to be arrogant nor to put their hope in wealth, which is so uncertain, but to put their hope in God, who richly provides us with everything for our enjoyment.
1 TIMOTHY 6:17

*W*hen you reverence Me and put Me first in your life, I will provide for you. Others around you may lack the necessities of life, but you will have all you need.

*Fear the Lord, you his saints, for those who fear him
lack nothing. The lions may grow weak and hungry,
but those who seek the Lord lack no good thing.*

PSALM 34:9,10

*G*ive, and it will be given to you. A good measure, pressed down, shaken together and running over, will be poured into your lap.

LUKE 6:38

A generous man will himself be blessed, for he shares his food with the poor.

PROVERBS 22:9

I will surely bless you, and I will surely multiply you.

HEBREWS 6:14 NAS

I will bless you...and you will be a blessing.

GENESIS 12:2

I will comfort you and protect you from harm. I will cause others to look upon you favorably. I will pour My blessings upon you as you trust Me and walk in My ways.

For the Lord God is a sun and shield;
the Lord bestows favor and honor; no good thing does he
withhold from those whose walk is blameless. O Lord
Almighty, blessed is the man who trusts in you.

PSALM 84:11,12

*W*hen you are diligent to study My Word and then apply it to your daily life, when you hear the Scriptures and keep your mind on them throughout your day, I am able to bless everything you do.

But he who looks carefully into the faultless law,
the (law) of liberty, and is faithful to it
and perseveres in looking into it, being not a heedless listener
who forgets, but an active doer (who obeys), he shall be
blessed in his doing—his life of obedience.
JAMES 1:25 AMP

When you remember how much I have forgiven you and the sacrifice Jesus made to pay for your sin, it's not difficult to keep offenses from taking root in your heart and to be merciful and forgiving to those who have hurt you.

Get rid of all bitterness, rage and anger...be kind and compassionate to one another, forgiving each other, just as in Christ God forgave you.
EPHESIANS 4:31,32

Do not become discouraged in doing what is right, for when the time is best, you will see abundant blessings because you persevered and did not quit.

Let us not become weary in doing good,
for at the proper time we will reap a harvest
if we do not give up.
GALATIANS 6:9

*C*hoose to trust Me and obey My Word and your life will overflow with My blessings. I will bless you in the city and in the country. Your children will be healthy and happy, and your food will bring nourishment to your body. You will be blessed wherever you go. I will help you over-come when others come against you. I will command My blessings upon your home, and everything you do will succeed. Everyone will see how I have blessed your life. I will give you abundant prosperity and I will bless the work of your hands. You will be the lender and not the borrower. I will make you a leader and not a follower. You will be a success and not a failure. This is the plan I have for you, My child, so choose a life of obedience and I will bring to pass all that I have promised.

DEUTERONOMY 28:1-13 (AUTHOR'S PARAPHRASE)

*L*ook, today I have set before you life and death, depending on whether you obey or disobey.... I call heaven and earth to witness against you that today I have set before you life or death, blessing or curse. Oh, that you would choose life; that you and your children might live!

DEUTERONOMY 30:15,19 TLB

*N*ow therefore listen to me, O you sons; for blessed—happy, fortunate to be envied—are those who keep my ways.

Proverbs 8:32 AMP

*D*o not give up your faith in Me to answer your prayers, for your trust will bring My miraculous power into your life. Have steadfast patience and endurance as you carry out My plan for you. Then you will receive all I have promised.

So do not throw away your confidence;
it will be richly rewarded. You need to persevere
so that when you have done the will of God,
you will receive what he has promised.
HEBREWS 10:35,36

I will protect you and give you peace of mind when you continually think of Me. Commit your whole heart to Me, and have confidence in what I have promised you, for I am the Lord your God, your everlasting strength.

You will guard him and keep him in perfect and constant peace whose mind...is stayed on you, because he commits himself to you, leans on you, and hopes confidently in you. So trust in the Lord...for the Lord God is an everlasting rock.
Isaiah 26:3,4 AMP

*D*o you realize how special you are to Me? You are always on My mind! I am continually thinking of you, all day and all night. Every morning when you wake up, I am still thinking about you!

How precious it is, Lord, to realize that you are thinking about me constantly! I can't even count how many times a day your thoughts turn toward me. And when I awaken in the morning, you are still thinking of me!
PSALM 139:17,18 TLB

*C*hange your life by meditating on My Word. Then you will understand and be certain of My will for every area of your life.

Be transformed by the renewing of your mind.
Then you will be able to test and approve what
God's will is—His good, pleasing and perfect will.
ROMANS 12:2

*I*t delights My heart when you put your faith in Me. I take great pleasure when you believe that I am real and that I will bless you as you diligently seek Me.

And without faith it is impossible to please God,
because anyone who comes to him
must believe that he exists and that he
rewards those who earnestly seek him.
HEBREWS 11:6

I knew you would receive My Son as your Lord and Savior before I created the world. Therefore I see you—pure and holy. Because of My great love for you, I adopted you as My child.

For he chose us in him before the creation of the world to be holy and blameless in his sight. In love he predestined us to be adopted as his sons through Jesus Christ.

EPHESIANS 1:4,5

Therefore I tell you, do not worry about your life, what you will eat or drink; or about your body, what you will wear. Look at the birds of the air; they do not sow or reap or store away in barns, and yet your heavenly Father feeds them. Are you not much more valuable then they? Do not worry, saying, "What shall we eat?" or "What shall we drink?" or "What shall we wear?" Your heavenly Father knows that you need them. But seek first His kingdom and His righteousness, and all these things will be given to you as well.

MATTHEW 6:25,26,31-33

134

Let me assure you that no one has given up anything—home, brothers, sisters, mother, father, children, or property—for love of me and to tell others the Good News, who won't be given back, a hundred times over, homes, brothers, sisters, mothers, children, and land—with persecutions! All these will be his here on earth, and in the world to come he shall have eternal life.

MARK 10:29,30 TLB

*W*hen you are aware that one of My children is not walking in obedience to My Word, pray for them, and I will give them life. Your prayers will be powerful and effective.

If anyone sees his brother commit a sin that does not lead to death, he should pray and God will give him life.
1 JOHN 5:16

The prayer of a righteous man makes tremendous power available—dynamic in its working.
JAMES 5:16 AMP

When you admit your sins to Me and ask for forgiveness, I will always forgive you. Then you will be totally clean and holy in My sight.

If we confess our sins, he is faithful and just
and will forgive us our sins and
purify us from all unrighteousness.

1 JOHN 1:9

I have wiped out your transgressions like a thick cloud, And your sins like a heavy mist. Return to me, for I have redeemed you.

ISAIAH 44:22 NAS

"Come now, let us reason together," says the Lord. "Though your sins are like scarlet, they shall be as white as snow; though they are red as crimson, they shall be like wool. If you are willing and obedient, you will eat the best from the land."

ISAIAH 1:18,19

*C*all to Me and I will defend you. When you have been falsely accused, I will come to your defense. Trust in Me, and I will come quickly to vindicate you and cause your righteousness to shine in the sight of all men.

And will not (our just) God defend and protect
and avenge his elect (his chosen ones)
who cry to him day and night? Will he defer them
and delay help on their behalf? I tell you, he will
defend and protect and avenge them speedily.
LUKE 18:7,8 AMP

*R*ejoice as you put your faith in Me, knowing that I will defend you. Let your heart fill with joy, realizing how I desire to bless your life. I will surround you with people who will highly respect and esteem you.

But let all those who put their trust in thee rejoice:
Let them ever shout for joy, because thou defendest them:
Let them also that love thy name be joyful in thee. For
thou, Lord, wilt bless the righteous; with favour wilt
thou compass him as with a shield.
PSALM 5:11,12 KJV

*R*est assured that the talents I have given you and the plan I have for your life will never be taken away. I will never remove them from you, nor will I change My mind. Your gifts and callings are given by My grace, and there is nothing you can say or do to eliminate them from your life.

For God's gifts and His call are irrevocable—
He never withdraws them when once
they are given, and He does not change His mind
about those to whom He gives His grace
or to whom He sends His call.
ROMANS 11:29 AMP

*A*ny temptation you face has been experienced by other people, so don't think you are unusual. You can trust Me; I will not allow a temptation in your life that you cannot handle. But when you are tempted, I will show you how to escape the power of it, so that you will be victorious.

No temptation has seized you except what is common to man. And God is faithful; he will not let you be tempted beyond what you can bear. But when you are tempted, he will also provide a way out so that you can stand up under it.

1 CORINTHIANS 10:13

$\mathcal{G}$ive me your heart, my son, and let your eyes delight in my ways.

PROVERBS 23:26 NAS

$\mathcal{M}$y son, if your heart is wise, then my heart will be glad; my innermost being will rejoice when your lips speak what is right.

PROVERBS 23:15,16

*T*hus says the Lord who made the earth, the Lord Who formed it to establish it...Call to Me and I will answer you and show you great and mighty things...you do not know.

JEREMIAH 33:2,3 AMP

Train your children by being a godly example in their lives. Teach them to follow Me, and when they have grown they will not depart from what you have taught them. If you do this, I promise to save your children and your grandchildren.

Train up a child in the way he should go:
and when he is old, he will not depart from it.
PROVERBS 22:6 KJV

But from everlasting to everlasting the Lord's love
is with those who fear him, and his righteousness
with their children's children.
PSALM 103:17

$\mathcal{Y}$our children will abide in My Word. I will teach and guide them by My Spirit. They will walk in My ways, and they will live in peace.

And all your (spiritual) children shall be disciples—
taught of the Lord (and obedient to his will); and great
shall be the peace and undisturbed composure
of your children.
ISAIAH 54:13 AMP

*T*hus says the Lord...I will pour My Spirit upon your offspring, and My blessing upon your descendents. And they shall spring up among the grass, as willows or poplars by the water courses. One shall say, I am the Lord's...another will write...upon his hand, I am the Lord's.

Isaiah 44:2–5 AMP

"As for me, this is my covenant with them," says the Lord. "My spirit, who is on you, and my words that I have put in your mouth will not depart from your mouth, or from the mouths of your children, or from the mouths of their descendants from this time on and forever," says the Lord.

ISAIAH 59:21

*Y*ou are always on My mind. I will bless you when you reverence My name. I will prosper you and your children as you put your trust in Me.

The Lord hath been mindful of us: he will bless us...
he will bless them that fear the Lord, both small
and great. The Lord shall increase you more and
more, you and your children.
PSALM 115:12–14 KJV

P. S. GOD LOVES YOU!

*D*o not worry about your children. I hear your prayers and I am at work within their hearts. Put your hope in My promise that your children will be saved from the enemy's hand and serve Me with all their hearts; for I will draw them to Myself with lovingkindness.

*Thus says the Lord: Refrain your voice from weeping,
and your eyes from tears; for your work shall be rewarded,
says the Lord; and (your children) shall return from the
enemy's land. And there is hope in your future,
says the Lord; your children shall come
again to their own country.*
JEREMIAH 31:16,17 AMP

When you put your faith in My Son Jesus, I entered into an agreement with you that cannot be broken, and this is what I promise to do: I will work within you, creating the desire and power to walk in My ways. I will delight in doing you good and giving you all the blessings I have promised.

They will be my people, and I will be their God. I will make an everlasting covenant with them: I will never stop doing good to them, and I will inspire them to fear me. I will rejoice in doing them good...[and] I will give them all the prosperity I have promised them.

JEREMIAH 32:38,40-42

*D*o not trust in your good works—feeling as though you have earned My blessings by something you have done. This will lead you to disappointment. But if you will keep your eyes on Jesus and trust all the promises that are yours because of Him, you will never be disappointed in your expectations.

They did not depend on faith but on what they could do—relying on the merit of their works. They have stumbled over the Stumbling Stone but he who believes in Him (who adheres to, trusts in and relies on Him) shall not be put to shame nor be disappointed in his expectations.

ROMANS 9:32,33 AMP

I have told you these things, so that in Me you may have perfect peace and confidence. In the world you have tribulation and trials and distress and frustration; but be of good cheer—take courage; be confident, certain, undaunted—for I have overcome the world.—I have deprived it of power to harm you, have conquered it (for you).

JOHN 16:33 AMP

*D*o not let your hearts be troubled...trust in and rely on God...and trust in and rely also on Me. Peace I leave with you; My (own) peace I now give...to you. Not as the world gives...Do not let your heart be troubled, neither let it be afraid—stop allowing yourselves to be agitated and disturbed; and do not permit yourselves to be fearful and intimidated and cowardly and unsettled.

JOHN 14:1,27 AMP

*D*on't worry about anything; instead, pray about everything; tell God your needs, and don't forget to thank him for his answers. If you do this you will experience God's peace, which is far more wonderful than the human mind can understand. His peace will keep your thoughts and your hearts quiet and at rest as you trust in Christ Jesus.

PHILLIPIANS 4:6,7 TLB

References

Other titles by Connie Witter include:

God's Great and Precious Promises
Love Letters from God

To contact the author, write:

Connie Witter
P. O. Box 3064
Broken Arrow, OK 74013-3064

Additional copies of this book are available from
your local bookstore.

Tulsa, Oklahoma 74155